RESPECT YOUR WIFE

PADHI

Title: Respect Your Wife
Author: Padhi
ISBN: 9789393606877
Paper Back First Edition: 2025

Instagram ID of the Author: @padhi.soumya

Published in India by:

2/42, 1st Floor, Ansari Road,
Darya Ganj, New Delhi – 110002.
Mobile No- 9958232447
E-Mail ID- emptycanvaspublishers@gmail.com

Foreword

A girl marries and becomes somebody's wife. She departs from her parental house with a vision to make her husband's house a perfect home. She struggles initially and succeeds subsequently. She sacrifices for her husband, children, and in-laws. This book is meant to make all realise her forgiveness, respect her hard work, praise her patience, and admire her talent. This handbook focuses more on the positiveness of a wife without deteriorating the definition of a husband. Through this book, I appeal to every husband in the world to respect his wife, respect her hard work, and respect her sacrifices. In return, you will get miracles.

A good husband makes a good wife.

-John Florio

She entered your life after the interval.
And believe me,
The second half is always interesting.

Who told me love happens only once? It can happen again. In my childhood, my first love was my mother. She, too, loved me unconditionally. After the arrival of my sibling, I observed her proportionate love towards both of us. After my marriage, my love life had shifted towards my wife and attraction towards my mother had started diminishing. The irony of Indian marriage is that the mother is always very keen on searching for a good match for her son or daughter and is ready to sacrifice her love for her kid's better half. This is the selfless sacrifice a mother often makes to keep her child happy.

Many of us might have engaged in immature love stories and indulged in many attachments, commitments, and situations before our marriage. Similarly, our spouse might have enjoyed her bachelorette world with someone she liked before. Relationship fails, love dies, and in turn, marriage is born. Marriage- the social structure that binds two individuals legally, mentally, emotionally, and physically.

Just like many Y-gens, I, too, drowned in love with my semi-ripen commitments. She, too, enjoyed my company in college. As soon as career options started rising in our minds, this relationship started fading away slowly. It does not mean we were not committed. The simple reason behind our separation was our career aspirations, financial ambitions, and social desires.

After struggling for some initial years in the job battle, I was convinced by my parents to get married. As I came from a middle-class family and had a decent income with no financial liabilities and commitments, my parents had only one expectation from me: to select one decent girl from those short-listed by them. I, too, visited some of those girls' houses after doing proper research on their social media activities and general enquiries with near and dears. Where I was very keen to marry, my parents took back foot, where they were comfortable, I didn't like that girl's appearance. For which girl we both liked, that girl had rejected me because of my transferable job. Finally, my parents and I came up with a proposal. That girl's family members interrogated me thoroughly, discussed it over the phone multiple times, and decided to proceed further.

Like any other Indian marriage, my marriage's verdict was too dependent on the astrologer's decree. As per the Hindu tradition, I had no other choice rather to agree with the elder's advice. Though we both got some time to speak to each other, we couldn't become familiar instantly. However, she had shown an early green signal, which forced me to say yes immediately. Parents had decided to start the rituals with engagement without any delay. Her father was also not ready to give any cooling period, rather convincing my father to fix the marriage date at the earliest. But somehow, I convinced her parents by stating my job profile and leave restrictions.

Our mobile numbers were shared officially. And we were free to talk to each other. It was the first Sunday. I was enjoying my weekend by sleeping after a heavy lunch. She rang me for the first time. Though the number was saved, I was not expecting her call so early. She started smoothly and asked about my daily routine, lifestyle, and office work culture, but the call got disconnected automatically after fifty-nine minutes. For the first time, I had talked with somebody so passionately and selflessly. Though I had spent many nights along with mosquitos while talking with my then-girlfriend, this time it was different. I was talking to my would-be wife. And I had decided to keep myself open to her genuine questions. I had become honest to her while answering all queries. And it's not only my story; it's a common story for many of us. We middle-class people have often failed in our first love but succeeded with our final one. Honestly disclosing, I love my wife. She entered into my life after the interval. I enjoyed my bachelorhood with childhood friends, college mates, and colleagues. However, attachment to her has a different era, a unique aura, and a beautiful aroma I had never come across in my life before marriage.

The journey between the engagement day and the wedding day taught me many things- mother is not your only selfless well-wisher, father is not your only influencer, brother is not your only supporter, and sister is not your only irritating partner. There is a variety of creature called 'wife', who fulfils your life, comes without any condition. Her temperament is nothing less than any mythological character; her attitude is nothing inferior to any Bollywood heroine, and her charisma is far better than any lady I have come across before.

I believe, most of us are very lucky to have such a beautiful support system with us. Till she entered our lives, we were in a monotonous mode. She sprinkles colours in our lives, spreads happiness in our minds, and puts smiles on our faces. Her appearance in our life has completed our individuality, given company to our thought process, shared our sorrows, and shattered our bad phases in life. Sometimes, she quarrels, argues, shouts, keeps her stand, and sticks to her principles.

But, believe me, friends, it's her drama for a while to put a break on our wrongdoings, our bad decisions, and scattered thinking. The reason behind this is for our betterment. So, enjoy her attachment and feel her magic in your life.

I'm a man of faith.
I only fear God,
And my wife - sometimes.

- Lech Walesa

Happy is the man who finds a true friend, and far happier is he who finds that true friend in his wife.

-Franz Schubert

A successful marriage requires falling in love many times, always with the same person.

-Mignon McLaughlin

Don’t compare her with your mother. She has a different role to play in your life.

In the *Mahabharat*, *Draupadi* had a different role. In the *Ramayan*, *Sita* had a separate role. In today's date, your wife has a specific role. She is the lead character in your life story. Your mother has nurtured you, made you capable of earning, and run your livelihood smoothly. But your wife has made your life larger. Her support system has added value to your overall performance.

Once we mature, our mother can only offer sympathy. But our wife provides us the strength to move forward, the courage to progress, and the vigour to prosper. Her selfless support in our daily routine can't be measured in any form, because it's uncountable.

She is responsive to all your frustrations, work pressure, and difficulties faced from the outside world. She is the only person who understands you better, stays within you, and tries to make you laugh at difficult times. In tough situations, she never takes the back foot but takes the rider's seat.

When we were children, our mother's love was felt deeply and compassionately, and our immature minds were trained based on her ideology. If the mother is devotional, the child usually goes to the temple frequently. If the mother is a singer, the child absorbs the singing quality easily. If the mother is good at studying, she gives her child the best education. The mother always tried to make you better than her, as she liked.

However, in the wife's case, it's different. The wife comes into our lives when our minds are mature. She can't change our already established ways of thinking. Rather, she can add value to make our mindset better than ever before. She never tries to change our thinking process instantly. She takes time to judge us. She plays the test match on our life's pitch. Slowly, she understands our intuition, our passion, our confrontation and our analysis with her philosophy. If she feels our mindset and way of thinking are better than hers, she customises herself rather than forcing us to change. In case we have some bad habits or have some wrong thinking, she will put her hundred percent into changing the same and bring our minds on the right track.

Since childhood till teenage, we got habituated with our mother’s homely food. After we moved out and stayed in hostel, we missed her special recipe. After getting job, we might have stayed as a paying guest or arranged a cook during our bachelorhood. During that particular phase, we have felt that our mother is the best cook for our tummy.

After marriage, we got accustomed to our better half's recipe. I have felt the development in my wife's cooking style, food preparation methods, plating presentation, etc. She customised her cooking style based on my food habits, likes, and dislikes. In turn, she sacrificed her food preparation methods. She might have changed her food habits because of mine. In this case, please note that our mother didn't forget her eating habits; rather, she made us habituated with her food choices. And we grew up with the same food intake.

Some people like plain shirts, some of us like colourful dresses, and many of us prefer casual outfits. All these dressing cultures we have adopted reflect our mother's selection towards our dressing sense. There is no doubt that she always prefers to make us smarter. But, at the same time, we too have gathered some fashion sense once we grew older. We came across many friends and colleagues having different taste in fashion, and tried changing our appearances, dress selections based on the circle we resided in our early twenties.

After our marriage, our wives might have tried to change our looks based on their likes, and we might have hesitated. Though she had irritated at first, gradually, she understood and enriched our way of dressing. Her suggestions have definitely attracted the attention of many colleagues. Overall, she never tries to make you look foolish or dull in front of others. Her only intention is to make you a complete man. Your mother, too, tried for the same. The only difference is that the mother has imposed the style on us, and the wife has transformed our sense of fashion.

In our college days, we liked to drive speedily and do late-night parties, but we never disclosed these to our mothers. Our mothers are very caring for us and, hence, usually keep some secrets about our bad doings. But we can't hide those same actions from our wives. They have the sixth sense to catch us. As we are staying in the same house and sharing the same room, we have become each other's first priority. Hence, we can't bluff our better halves for all our stupid things.

Our mothers can shout at us for waking up late, if we are not taking a bath on time every day, and not eating quality food timely. We, too, have got irritated many times, and heated arguments have happened. Unlikely, in the wife's case, she understands our situation, choices, preferences and tries to make us better people with good habits by politely convincing us. As our relationships grew older, our understandings became stronger. She got that advantage by knowing our weak points and tried to customise our habits. In turn, we have gradually become good human beings. Therefore, we should thank our wives for giving us rebirth and for making us a better person. Their little impact on our lifestyle has changed our mindset, enhanced our positivity, and boosted our personality.

At any point of time, our mothers can't be compared with our wives. They both have different roles in our lives at different junctures. Both are equally important for us. We should avoid comparison between them rather than manage equilibrium between their preferences. In my opinion, a good son can be a good husband. Similarly, a good wife can be a good daughter-in-law. It purely depends on our thought process and how we react to both of them. And believe me, if they both become good friends, we can definitely enjoy our lives on behalf of their support system.

A good wife is one who serves her husband in the morning like a mother does, loves him in the day like a sister does and pleases him like a prostitute in the night.

-Chanakya

All you need for happiness is a good gun,
a good horse,
and a good wife.

-Daniel Boone

She might be messy,
but she wants to make you classy.

Every individual has its own thought process, own lifestyle, own way of living. Changing anybody's daily routine takes some time, especially when he or she is matured enough. Because, infants observe and learn from their parents. But, once the child grows older, moulding his or her lifestyle is a little bit difficult. Same thing happens with our spouse.

After our marriage, my wife came to my house. She took sometime to settle down. She got engaged in many jobs. Small small things had occupied her time. She tried a lot to accustom with our house's work culture, daily routine. She tried to make us happy in maximum aspects. At the same time, she forgot to give time to herself. As an individual, she had her own preference. She had sacrificed her happiness for our family's comfort.

She could have imposed her way of thinking on us. But, she preferred to follow our family's culture, tradition, and customs. She is the only daughter of her parents. Before marriage, she had never made her bed, she had never cleaned utensils, and she had not swept the floor very often. Her mother was helping her to keep her clothes properly. She did not get the chance to cook food in her house. After marriage, she came to our house where most of the daily chores were new for her.

She followed her mother's advice and put her extra effort into making our family happy. She customised her lifestyle. From morning to evening, she followed all daily routines as per our habits. Her toothpaste, soap, and shower gel brands had been changed. In her house, she was wearing shorts. After marriage, she couldn't, because of my parents' conservative approach. She had forgiven her heels because of my short height. She had reduced her junk food habits, started liking non-vegetarian foods, and reduced her spicy intake. At the same time, she forgot to make the bed, put her wet clothes outside after bath, place her shoes inside the shoe rack, switch off lights and fans when nobody was there in any room, keep her make-up essentials in my shavings kit, used my comb and her pulled hairs were stuck on it.

These situations are not only faced by me alone. We all might have faced these in our early marriage life. Many of us might have influenced by our mother to point out her minute mistakes. Our conservative approach might have hurt her sentiments. She might have cried hard because of our foolish immature reaction for such tiny things. In this regard, I express that if we compare her sacrifice for us and for our family members, her messy things are very diminutive and should be excused.

Every wife wants to see their husband as the best in the world. Generally, we men are not so much comparative in nature, particularly in looks, get-ups, and appearances. However, our wives try to make us look handsome. Which dress to wear on what occasion, shirt or t-shirt, shoe or sneaker, colour combination, wear sun glass or not etc. are decided by our spouse.

As a lady, a wife has always some fashion sense. I believe that women are better when it comes to appearance. They always give importance to their looks. And therefore, they, too, prefer to make their husbands more appealing. I have often hesitated to wear printed shirts during our vacation days. Because I always prefer a formal dress or a plain polo collar T-shirt. Somehow, she convinced me to wear colourful shirts that she had purchased. I prefer a clean shave every day. But she advised me to keep a little beard that suits my face. Initially, I was reluctant. Slowly, I followed her advice and got appreciation from my colleagues. My shared photographs on social media have got likes and comments because of her dressing preferences for me.

After engaging herself in many household things, she has forgotten to give time to herself, her ownness, her skincare, her hair care, and her body. So, each Sunday, we should give her some free time. We or our family members should take care of our kids. She should feel relaxed on Sundays or any holidays so that she can concentrate on her personal things. In fact, there is nothing personal. But we all want our wives to look beautiful. Just like she was, in our first vacation photographs. In case our conservative family members raise their eyebrows, it's our duty to convince them. Because it's the payoff time for our wives. She is not demanding anything extraordinary; rather, we should voluntarily support her. We should help her by dropping her off at the park, parlour, kitty parties, etc. If she gets two to three hours for herself on the weekend, she will be happier and more dedicated to our household work on weekdays. In the end, her happiness matters for our peace of mind.

The husband who decides to surprise his wife is often very much surprised himself.

-Voltaire

Behind every successful man is a proud wife and a surprised mother-in-law.

-Hubert H. Humphrey

Dear wife,
A sea of whisky couldn’t intoxicate me
as a drop of you.

–JS Parker

She is in your nest.
So, be honest.

All marriages in the world start with a beautiful beginning. Slowly, it matured. For some people, it got rusted early. For many of us, love and affection were diluted because of family priorities. During the earlier days of our marriage, we might have promised many things. Just like any Indian family drama movie, our mindset was colourful during our marriage. We were very possessive about our wife. We pretended to be dedicated during the first year of marriage. Slowly, our minds shifted towards careers, income and children. Even parents' extra intervention in everything has ruined many good relationships.

Though the love marriage's percentage has been increasing day by day, the marriage rituals are happening just like a traditional marriage. Because we are Indians, our first thought process is, *What will people say? What will our neighbour say? What will our relatives say?* To show up to them and make the marriage a grand celebration, we have been spending a lot of our hard-earned money. I have come across many occasions where parents have availed loans against properties, and the boy or girl has availed personal loans from banks to spend lavishly to showcase a grand wedding. Except for that, the dowry system has not been fully eradicated from our culture. Only, it's converted as declared gifts. The girl's father is making separate savings for his boy's study purpose and the girl's marriage purpose. Even after a good career and decent job profile of an Indian girl, her father spends a lot in marriage. To support the culture, even our government has been focusing more on higher interest for deposits in the name of girl children and women. Sukanya Samriddhi Scheme and Mahila Samman Yojana are examples that resemble the same.

After spending a lot and sacrificing her parents and their first family, she entered our family. Till the date of marriage, she had a free life. She enjoyed her ownness, commanded her father, shouted at her mother, and fought with her brother for some silly things. Suddenly, her lifestyle has changed. In the modern nuclear family, parents stay separately, the marriage rituals take around one month, and she has to face the consequences. She has to wear a *saree*, put a *pallu* or *dupatta* on her head, use *sindoor*, and talk slowly, nicely, smilingly, and forcefully with relatives, near and dear ones.

Once marriage is over, she is in your nest. She will use your bedroom, your wardrobe, your bathroom, your mirror. She may switch off the air conditioner at night, which you usually put on, and use a blanket. She may switch on the bed light at night, which you have never used earlier. She will keep your dresses nicely, making space for hers in the wardrobe. She will keep her make-up items in front of your dressing table. She will make your bed nicely, change the bed sheet frequently, and put the window screen properly. If she is a homemaker, she may watch daily soaps on television and discuss her favourite character with you. You may not like her routines. But, you should respond to her feelings.

You might have some bad habits like drinking or smoking. She definitely will not entertain all these routines. So, it's your duty to forgive your bad habits. Like a best friend, she will convince you to refrain from such addictions. If you don't change easily, she will follow a stricter approach. After all, she wants you to become healthy.

You might have any girlfriend before your marriage, any affairs might be with your lady colleagues. The same should be stopped with immediate effect. If you find it difficult to draw a line on your past relationship, its better to change the mobile number, change the employer, change the city. In case you are in public sector entities, and unable to change so, then you have no other option rather restrict yourself from such connections.

Be honest with your wife. Now you are married. You have got your marriage certificate. Posted your couple photos on social media. Everybody in your friend circle came to know about your new life. If you have any past affairs, it is better to inform your wife well in advance. Don't keep anything secret. She is mature enough to understand your feelings. She should realise that the past is past, and she is the only priority for you at present. Similarly, she might have some past story. Suppose she shares, well and good. If she reserves, don't ask her annoyingly. Better wait for the correct time. If she feels you have come closer, she will definitely share her past with you. So, be truthful in your relationship. Don’t be a detective of her character. If any of your family members try to become a detective on your wife's personality, just ignore him or her.

You are the husband. You married her. You should be the first option for her with whom she can share everything. This closeness should be earned by you and gained by your dedication, honesty, and passion towards her lifestyle.

To gain such closeness, you should give time to her and listen to her good, bad, ugly, and naughty things. Her mischief should be attended to. Her goodness should be felt. All your reactions should be honest. You should not sugarcoat your feelings for her. It should be hundred percent true, natural and genuine. Your honesty can only buy her happiness. In turn, her happiness will shape a good family, your own family- i.e. you, your wife, your children. Soon, your home will become heaven.

There are three faithful friends –
An old wife,
An old dog,
And ready money.

-Benjamin Franklin

You don't love someone
because they're perfect;
you love them
in spite of the fact that
they're not.

–Jodi Picoult

When you find the one that's right for you, you feel like they were put there for you; you never want to be apart."

–Joe Manganiello

Prioritise her happiness.
It rewards a lot.

A happy mind delivers good results. Likewise, a happy wife makes a happy home. Happiness comes from satisfaction. Happiness comes from good surroundings. Happiness comes from positive vibes. Happiness depends upon the percentage of achievement that meets expectations.

Every individual has different choices and preferences. After marriage, the couple get customised to each other's liking. To make the better half happy, the husband and wife have to sacrifice some of his or her habits and preferences. In our Indian context, a wife generally sacrifices more than a husband. She has to sacrifice her house, where she spent most of her life till marriage. She has to sacrifice her parents, who have nurtured her. She has to sacrifice her siblings with whom she fought a lot and shared her moments. She came out of her comfort zone and decided to marry.

Wife comes to our home. We welcome her like a goddess. As a part of Hindu rituals, she starts cooking on the second day. And it never stops after that. Her work portfolio increases slowly and steadily. From cooking to cleaning, maintaining to memorising, feeling to fulfilling, she becomes the centre of all household work.

She engages herself in all minute works and gives a little time to herself. Her personal time gets squizzed after marriage. Her preferences changes from herself to her family well-being. Her family, means our family. She adjusts herself in all odd situations and tried to maintain equilibrium between her ego and family's respect.

Many times I have come across, where my wife has forgotten to iron her dress. But, at the same time, she ensures perfect dressing for our kid. She ignores to make her hair, but make our child's hair before dropping him to school everyday. She packs our lunch boxes nicely, but gulps in a single plate hurriedly.

What I observed that, after marriage my wife has sacrificed her happiness to make me happy, our family happy. Her priorities have been shifted based on my parents' expectations, my kid's requirement and off course, my preferences. She has lost herself in bundle of works and forgotten to give time to herself.

She never prioritises her happiness. She always thinks for others. Therefore, we as a husband should respect her hard labour, sacrifices and give priority to her happiness. She might be good at singing or dancing or painting before marriage. She might be wanted to participate in reality shows, she might have interested on short videos like Instagram Reels, YouTube Shots. She might have interest in cooking, travelling, photography. We should understand her likings, and pursue accordingly.

In her opinion, she is a good singer. But, you don't like her singing style. It’s not matching with the original voice. Don’t worry. Just encourage her. Don’t demoralise on her face. She is not going to get any awards. She sings or dances to express her emotions and to come out of busy household routines. We may suggest her for betterment, but politely, not always. Always poking her about her hidden talent demoralises her intuition.

She may like to eat outside once in a week or once in a fortnight. Just go with her. Because, the cook is never fond of her dishes. Similarly, after cooking every day for all family members, your wife may not like the same taste. So, if she wants to go out for a taste change, you better go with her. She may be satisfied with a single *Samosa* or a plate of *Momo*. Sometimes, she may try South Indian dishes like *Dosa*, *Idli*, *Uttapam*, etc. To make her happy, you should take to her favourite restaurant or food stall. She knows about your financial capacity. So, she will definitely check the price of any dish before ordering the same. There, too, she restricts herself. Just imagine if she is not able to eat as she chooses. Therefore, after mingling with her for some months, you should order her favourite food and take her to her favourite hangout place before she requests.

The day you come to know about her weaknesses and her cravings, you should fulfil her wants. Her feelings should be satisfied, her preferences should be heard. In turn, she will try to keep you happier than before. She will be more dedicated to your priorities and well-being.

In some cases, her priorities and yours may not match. Her food preferences may not match with yours. She may like spicy food, you may like non-spicy, she may like gravy, you may not, she may like rice, you may like *roti*. She prefers vegetarian food, and your favourite is non-vegetarian dishes. In such cases, she never compels you to shift to her food habits. In a similar manner, you should never force her to change her food habits. In the Hindu calendar, there are so many *pujas* and auspicious days on which women should eat vegetarian foods without onion or garlic. On such occasions, you, too, have to restrict yourself from non-vegetarian foods and obey your wife’s command. She is doing *puja* for your well-being and your family's well-being. She takes a bath early in the morning, visits a temple, and worships God. All those sacrifices are for you. Therefore, respect her dedication, support her decisions, and prioritise her happiness.

Please note that a happy wife can make miracle in our life. Her happiness is a blessings for us. Her priorities should be respected, given importance, for making a happy home, a beautiful family.

A happy wife is a happy life.

-Gavin Rossdale

If I had just one wish,
my lovely wife,
I would choose to spend
the rest of my days with you.

-Unknown

Passion is a word which involves
so many feelings.
I feel it when we touch,
I feel it when we kiss,
and I feel it when I look at you.
You are my passion—my one true love.

–S Richardson

God has sent her for your betterment.
So, respect her work.

We grew older along with our parents. Our siblings, too, grew with us. Our friends also grew with us. We have adapted many new things, customised many of our characteristics, and motivated us towards some positive vibes and influential people. We changed ourselves slowly and steadily based on what our environment needed from us.

In the middle of our life span, our wife-like support system was gifted by our parents. She entered into our lives, created a positive ambience, and started doing miracles in daily routines. After her appearance, we felt relaxed. We felt like somebody came to us to share our works, emotions, and feelings in the long run. She, too, came with some mindset and expectations. After a decade of my marriage, I understood that a wife never comes with any condition. Her only requirement is compassion. She wants some pampering and buttering to light her mind. Her hard work needs support, both physically and mentally. She may have a lot of discrepancies between your mother and herself, which can be eradicated by your little partiality towards her. She should feel that you are with her, you are beside her, and you are behind her.

Life as it grows old teaches us many lessons. Similarly, I realised a wife's sacrifice when it comes to my struggle with blood cancer. My mother had given sympathy. My father had given me money. My brother had supported me in transportation. But my wife had supported me during the bad phase. She walked with me. Stayed as an attendant in the hospital cubicle. She cleaned my sweat, wiped my back, and flushed the toilet. Every day was a rebirth for me. My father was planning for life insurance policies. My mother was praying to God. But she was spending sleepless nights along with me in the hospital ward.

It was just ten months into my marriage when I was diagnosed with blood cancer. She had the option to leave me. She had the option to start a new family with somebody. But she had decided to stay with me. Still, I remember her dialogue, "I can't leave you in the middle. I will make you fit; it's my promise." Her dedication, hard work, and patience gave me a rebirth. Even though I had no confidence in myself that I would be all right, her dedication saved my life. After struggling for six months in a hospital bed, I recovered.

She had sacrificed her professional career growth because of my health issues. She had decided to stay with me, always, forever. I had no bad habits. And I continued to restrict my diet based on the doctor's advice. During my tour days, she cooked food and packed in a tiffin, even at 4 am in the morning, so that I could avoid outside food.

She packs my bag when I go for an official tour. She ensures that everything is packed. There is no scope for any outside food or borrowing things. Even when we travel together, she ensures the same for me and my son. As a result, we stay fit and save some amount. Some of my friends have mocked at me and criticised me as a miser. But, I ignored the same by realising that my wife is smarter than anybody in the world.

During our visit to Leh, I was struggling to breathe due to lack of oxygen in the air. She, too, felt the same. But, at the same time, she helped me feel better, went to a nearby medicine store, brought the required first aid, and supported me in feeling better. In turn, I couldn't help her, rather ordered her for a head massage. She, too, pampered me for a better sleep. Like this, many live examples I have come across where I realised that a dedicated wife sacrifices more than any husband.

During any travel journey, the wife takes care of the child. The husband takes care of the luggage. Taking care of fixed assets is always easier than caring for a living object. So, don't think that we have been doing a great job by carrying luggage. She packs food, packs dress, packs medicines, makes your child ready, naps him or her twice a day, and takes him or her to the toilet. We only do easy works, simple works. All minute jobs in our family are usually done by our wives.

Always respect her hard work. She has been dedicated to your life and your family members' well-being. As a messenger of God, she always does miracles. Her words heal our hearts, and her works mend our bodies. In return, she never expects anything precious. She only needs acknowledgement for her hard work and her dedication. We should feel her acknowledged. Only then she will be accomplished in her vision. Her only vision is to make all happy. She never thinks anything negative about you, your child, or your parents. Her anger may be for a short period, her sadness is for a particular moment. In the end, she loves you. She respects you. She may give more importance to your kid rather than you because she is the creator. In fact, you both are the manufacturers of your child. So, she becomes possessive towards your child rather than on you.

We Indians have belief on God. And remember, she is the incarnation of Goddess. We have been imploring her many times, knowingly or unknowingly. She too sprinkles happiness on our faces without any imparity. She is really great.

Love is not about possession.
Love is about appreciation.

- Osho

There's this place in me
where your fingerprints still rest,
your kisses still linger,
and your whispers softly echo.
It's the place where a part of you
will forever be a part of me.

–Gretchen Kemp

**Love is of all passions the strongest,
for it attacks simultaneously the head,
the heart, and the senses.**

–Lao Tzu

The conversation may lead to an argument. It can be controlled by your judgement, your attachment, and your temperament.

Every individual has a specific type of ego at a certain point of time. Ego are of different types – id, ego, super ego. These are three different, functionally interlocking main components of the human soul, as investigated and defined by Sigmund Freud. Ego too has different stages like Adult, Critical Parent, Over-Nurturing

Parent, Adolescent and Child Heart. Ego states continue to develop throughout a person's life, but different ego states dominate at different times.

For satisfying anybody's ego, he or she may go to any extent. For an individual, self respect is utmost important. Like wise our wives also have their own way of thinking, own style of approach, own ego state. For understanding these ego states, here I am going to put a glimpse about various unhealthy ego states.

Unhealthy Ego States are Selfish, Pleaser, Rebellious, Master Manipulator, Critical, and Enabling.

Selfish – In the selfish ego state, people are reckless and demanding. They try to have fun without thinking of the consequences.

Pleaser – People who are pleasers obey the rules, but do not necessarily believe in the rules. They are obedient in the hopes of flying under the radar. They are more concerned with looking like a good person than being a good human being.

Rebellious – The opposite of the pleaser is rebellious. Rebellious people are openly oppositional. They resent and reject control by others. Also, they reject the ideas of cooperation or compromise with others.

Manipulator – Manipulators have no regard for rules that get in the way of their own interests. They will exaggerate, distort the truth, or try to play psychological games with others. They intend to serve themselves at the expense of others.

Critical – Critical people try to control others by being demanding or judgmental. They may also use sarcasm. The intention is to dominate other people.

Enabling – People who are enabling, try to eliminate other people's suffering in order to make themselves feel more comfortable. They feel, it's their responsibility to make other people happy or successful. While enabling people believe that they are being nurturing, the message they send to others is that, other people are not capable of caring for themselves.

After years of marriage, spending most of our time with our better half, we can easily fit her in any of these above mentioned ego states. In some particular moment, she may also be fitted in more than one ego states.

Conversations happen between a husband and a wife more often. It's a good sign for a healthy family. Conversation opens up each other's individual feelings. At last, it may lead to some conclusions. Sometimes, no outcome is released from a conversation. Sometimes, the conversation may lead to an argument. The reason behind such an argument is any of these ego states, as mentioned in above paragraphs.

Argument happens only if the ego states are matching with each other. In this regard I draw your attention that if both husband and wife are selfish, argument happens. If one in the pair is selfish, the other is accepting his or her selfishness and accommodating accordingly, then they can continue as a happy couple. And this example is applicable for all these above mentioned unhealthy ego states.

Many happy families get spoiled due to a match between individuals' ego states. Some couples get derailed due to their immediate reactions. After marriage, it's the universal law that one person has to bend down a little so that the relationship will flow without any hurdles. However, in the new age, couples are not accepting this divine law of nature and are trying to justify themselves that they are right, which means each individual is right in his or her place. The husband says he is right, and the wife says she is right. At last, who will decide who is right?

If we think- time will decide, time will heal, then time will flow, and we will lose those moments in our lives. Then, what is the solution? We should find out. The resolution of any ego clash is to stop the argument. Many times, the discussion gets heated up due to arguments. Arguments are never considered to be a constructive element in our life. It destroys happiness, spoils valuable time, and damages intellectual thinking. Therefore, try to minimise your reaction. If wife is saying something due to anger, better listen to her. When she calms down, try to explain to her, analyse her. She will listen and understand. She reacts in anger due to work pressure. Nowadays, a wife has to compete in the office, fight for promotion, and give time to colleagues along with household work. Just like a pressure cooker, she bursts due to inner pressure and work overload.

It's our duty to help her in daily household chores. We men can give some time to our child, his or her home works, parent-teacher meetings. If we play with our kid every evening, our bond will become stronger. Wife will get some free time to catch up with her parents, relatives and friends. Her half an hour leisure time will boost her productivity.

Some days, she may carry unnecessary tensions from her office. Her boss might have trolled her. She will react in home. In such situation, just absorb her actions, don't show any reaction in front of your child. You should control your anger, control your mouth. Just remember the movie scene of *Thappad*, where one slap had ruined one relationship badly.

It's all about our attachment. How we understand her pain, her feelings. If she is hurt by outside pressure, she will react in front you. Because, you are closer to her heart than anybody else. Your action, your sympathy, your belongingness will massage her mind, heal her heart.

Love is not weakness.
It is strong.
Only the sacrament of marriage
can contain it.

– Boris Pasternak

Happy is the man
who finds a true friend,
and far happier is he who finds
that true friend in his wife.

– Franz Schubert

**She is not a graveyard.
Rather, she is a vineyard.
So, explore her eternal beauty
by compassionating her.**

Love creates human beings. Wife creates husband. Marriage is only a stepping stone. It's the approach of both individuals to make their marriage a successful one. Success can't be measured. It can only be felt. If both are happy with each other, then the marriage can be assumed as successful. If any counterpart is not happy, not satisfied, or not pleased with the other's approach, then he or she can't be a happy person.

There is no such specific *mantra* for making the marriage and relationship happy. No philosopher has invented any recipe for a successful relationship. After analysing deeper, I found that all failures, separated *gurus*, have become so-called philosophers. They couldn't succeed in love. They couldn't make their spouse happy. Now they are teaching the whole world how to keep your family happy. They might have learnt from their mistakes. But, without any practical experience, any intellectual person can't guide you on how to make your relationship live.

After studying hard, getting a good job, getting a better pay package, what we have achieved in our lives? Nothing special. Slowly, our happiness has been fading away with corporate work pressure. Our personal time has been snatched by mobile phones. Our holidays have been booked by office backlogs. Compared to our parents, we are more focused on our job profile, not our family matters. Our parents didn't have much career aspirations. Their only ambition was to educate us so that we could get a decent job. But, in our case, we have been planning for our bigger second house, our third foreign tour in a year, a luxury four-wheeler, dinner in a five-star restaurant, etc.

In the need hierarchy stated by Abraham Maslow, our parents had aimed for safety need and we are trying for our esteem needs. And in this rat race, we have been sacrificing our peace of mind, our personal time, our family time. As a working woman, many of our wives also have been customised their lifestyle. They have been joggling between personal and professional preferences.

Money is important in life. Double income gives cushion to a family's lifestyle. Women empowerment should be promoted. Wife's ambition should be respected, supported. We have been motivated by all these words. Women are tempted towards corporate work culture because of social status, freestyle living and ended up in chaos due to undue work pressure, both from home and office.

What I have observed is that, a working lady gives priority to office work and sacrifices some percentage of household routines. Though she is emotionally attached to her child, she is not able to spend much time with him or her. Office timings have been elongated gradually. As you grow up on the corporate ladder, eight hours duly grows to twelve hours. Two hours a day, any human being needs for himself or herself. Seven to eight hours of sleep is mandatory for a working brain. Then, there is hardly any time left in our daily routine for the next generation. The leisure times have been hijacked by mobile phones. A nuclear family gets time to dine together only on Sundays. Due to changes in lifestyle and city traffic, dinner time has slowly been delayed from 9 pm to 11 pm in major cities. Early to bed, early to rise concept has been eradicated by various Instagram influencers. They have so much advice to boost your mind and body, and sleeping time has become an optional subject.

As a lady, any wife always wants to give her hundred percent, both in the office and at home. In reality, it ended up in chaos; frustration comes out when not getting a promotion on time. She gets distracted, frustrated, evaporated and starts reacting to small, silly things at home. As she is earning and contributing to household necessities, we should respect her hard work and give her the courage to continue her effort rather than introspecting her delay in promotion. We should not discuss her negative things or her failures in front of her. She will feel embarrassed and demoralised.

We should always remember that, her mental strength is of utmost importance for our family's survival. She is not a graveyard, so all bad things will be buried in her mind. Rather, she is a vineyard who produces sweetness and calmness for our goodness. Just like a Genie lamp creates magic, if we rub her shoulder and pamper her back, she will sprinkle smiles and spread happiness around us. And if she is happy, we are happy. In turn, the happiest mind delivers the best work assigned to him or her.

For any husband, her wife should be the prettiest among all women he comes across. He should love her eternal beauty, respect her everlasting affection, be passionate about her emotion, and be compassionate about her passion. For two-thirds of our lifespan, we are going to spend time with our wives. She, too, is going to spend her maximum lifespan with us. To make the life journey smoother, affection for each other creates lubrication. That lubricant polishes our thought process, smoothens our mind, and enlightens our intuition.

Encouragement gives motivation. Motivation influences effort. Effort transforms action. Action delivers results. Good encouragement is essential for getting better results. Therefore, always encourage your wife. Promote her ambition. Engage with her to start. Support in her journey towards success. Forgive her wrongdoings, forget her failures. Aim on her goal. She is already giving her best. Only your little positiveness will bring a smile to her face. Happily, she will perform. And we all know, happy minds perform better. Likewise, she will be a super mom, super colleague, super woman if and only if you stand with her, support her, and compassionate her.

Love is the condition in which the happiness of another person is essential to your own.

- Robert A. Heinlein

If you live to be a hundred,
I want to live to be a hundred minus one day
so I never have to live without you.

- A.A. Milne

**A happy marriage doesn't mean
you have a perfect spouse
or a perfect marriage.
It simply means,
you've chosen to look beyond
the imperfections in both.**

– Fawn Weaver

For her, intelligence comes after emotion.

Intelligence comes from mind. Emotion comes from heart. Emotions are an inbuilt part of any animal. With learning and experience, intelligence develops. Intelligence can be positive or negative. It can have various motives. It can have complexities. Whereas, emotion is pure.

A mind can be diluted, but a heart can't. The heart is always genuine and tender towards good people. The heart follows the flow, whereas the mind follows instinct. Mind reads other's mind. Heart feels other's heart. Smile resides in the heart; attitude resides in the mind. In this artificial intelligence era, intelligence alone has no value. What we value is a pure heart with an intelligent mind. Intelligent people with progressive thought processes have always been rewarded in modern history, and negative mindsets have been destroyed in the past. Therefore, affection has more weight than intelligence.

In the present scenario, we have been following our job lives meticulously for survival in the social race. In our busy schedules, we give less importance to values, ethics, and living with our temperament. Due to high work pressures in white-collar jobs, our blood sugar levels have been shooting up drastically. If both husband and wife are on the job, then they have already spoiled their health, and now it's the turn for their child. To come out of such a scenario, we should always give some time to ourselves. We should close our bathroom door, stand in front of the mirror and talk to ourselves- *Are we happy with our job? Are we happy with our family? Is everything moving smoothly between us and our better halves?* Definitely not yes for all these questions. But, there is only one constant. We work for our family. We love our family.

In general, the male member gets irritated more often due to undue workload. The female member maintains the equilibrium at home by sharing her husband's household work. The working female member never expects any special things from her husband, rather tries to smooth line both of their day-to-day activities. A homemaker always maintains a good atmosphere at home. She never reacts easily, never shouts often, and she never blames her fate simply. She is mature enough to understand the meaning of life, the relationship between husband and wife.

Nowadays, all advice is available freely on social media. Anybody who has a mobile phone with a data pack is carrying the whole world's encyclopaedia. Therefore, we should not underestimate any homemaker, we should not underrate any housewife, and we should not undervalue any wife's intelligence. She has been upgrading her knowledge by staying at home, watching informative videos, and discussing with her friends, neighbours, and parents. But she never shows off her brainpower in front of her husband. She would rather use those in teaching her child.

She is committed to you. So, she communicates through her heart, not through her brain. She prefers to accept you as you are, without any filter, without any modification, without any customisation on your character, on your personality. She loves you without any condition. For her, emotion is the priority. Emotion can be happiness, sadness, disgust, fear, surprise, anger, pride, shame, embarrassment, or excitement. As a wife, she can adapt any incarnation of emotion based on the situation. Because she is not a superwoman, rather a normal human being. Her emotional attachment reflects the strength of our relationship.

As we grow older, we have started sacrificing many things, forgiving many characters. Similarly, she has forgiven many of our bad attitudes, behaviours, past histories. We have also been acquainted with her emotional drama and started to adapt her reactions easily, smoothly. Because, we as a husband have to sacrifice at some point of time so that our family life will run effortlessly.

We Indians were living in a male-dominated society where women were running the house, growing children, and we were earning for livelihood. Slowly, we have been developing. Our society has started giving equal importance to women. The Wife's work portfolio has been ever-increasing. So, her emotional drama has also been increasing. If we start comparing her emotions with her productivity, we are far behind her. She tells, listens, instructs, works, advises, and accepts. But in our case, we men are not accepting our weaknesses easily. Our temperament has created barriers to our good communication. We are using our brains for many negative things instead of using them to understand our inner world.

To understand any wife's inner world, we should emotionally attach with her. We should keep our intellectual minds aside, sit beside her, and talk to her. She should feel our openness towards her. Then only she will open up, slowly, passionately. She will share her emotions, we will share ours. She will cry, we will wipe her tears. We will cry, she will pamper on our back. She will get angry, we should listen to her voice. We will be angry, she will absorb our words. Then only we can make a good home, a happy home. A home where she will keep aside her intelligence, and we will respect her emotions. Our child will gain motivation.

The love we have in our youth
is superficial compared to the love
that an old man has for his old wife.

-Will Durant

**To love or have loved, that is enough.
Ask nothing further.**

- Victor Hugo

Marriage is like
watching the color of leaves in the fall;
ever changing and more stunningly beautiful
with each passing day.

– Fawn Weaver

**She is the creator of your home,
manufacturer of your child,
and caretaker of your parents.**

House is just a physical structure. It can be owned by anybody. Whereas home is more than just brick and mortar. Creating a home is making a space that is uniquely ours, that expresses us and how we want to live our life. And most importantly, it helps us to bring our family members together, creating memories that will be cherished forever.

For converting a house to home, women have a lead role to play. My mother had created our home. My wife has converted my flat into a home. They have customised everything inside the house, they felt each corner of the house, they fixed all furniture, fixture as per our family members' requirement.

Ladies are good home makers. We can only buy a house. We can supplement to their ideas for a better home. We can contribute to their good memories inside those four walls. We can spend good times with our better halves in our home. After a hectic schedule, when I return from office, I feel relaxed in my home. Because, life rests at home, mind naps at home, heart heals at home.

Whenever I am on an official tour, I can't sleep properly in a hotel room. The reason behind this is my acquaintance with my bedroom. The five-star restaurant's best cuisine is not at par with our own homemade dishes. Seating on the sofa in our living room while watching the cricket match gives more pleasure than watching a superstar's movie in an unknown theatre.

Comfort is felt at home. Happiness is shot at home. And reason behind the same is our wives. Their dedication, hard work and magic touches make our home unique. From morning to evening, they have been continuing their great works. They have been contributing more than any of our family members towards our home in a selfless manner, without expecting anything in return.

A wife always contributes. A good wife contributes more in better ways. A great wife understands our expectations and delivers accordingly. She completes our necessities, fulfils our wants, and satisfies our desires. Because of her love, affection, and kindness, we feel relaxed in our home.

The purpose of marriage in not only to stay happy, become each other's companion. The other reason is reproduction, create the next generation of our family. A wife plays a vital role in doing so. She takes the pain, patiently waits for nine months and gives birth. A family completes after a couple becomes parents.

Becoming a mother is not an easy task. Within that nine-month period, a wife has to experience a lot of mood swings. A husband should be beside her and support her both mentally and physically. When all family members are excited to welcome the newborn, the mother will be in post-delivery complications. Her wounds won't heal quickly. Her body may not produce milk immediately. During such an initial period of motherhood, the husband's support is very much essential. In a joint family, there is always some sort of support from experienced family members. However, in a nuclear family, it's the utmost priority of the husband to take care of his wife as well as the child. Even in a normal delivery, the wife's body needs time to heal. During such period, the husband should opt for paternity leave and take care of his wife. Once the wife heals, the mother's character comes out of her body. She will give more time to the child than her husband. Her working style will be prioritised for her baby, and all other works will take the back seat.

Sometimes, I personally feel that, my son gets more importance than me in my house. He is my son, our only son. Thinking those, I am accepting my down gradation, and enjoying family time lively. My wife has been possessive about our son and started quarrelling with me because of his future, his benefit, his lifestyle. I have no other option rather accepting her over-protectiveness and feel happy from inner sense.

After our parents grew older, they became dependent on us. They have taken care of us when we were children. Now, it's our turn to take care of them in their old age. Parents means both of our parents, wife's and husband's. In an Indian family, the parents word is still restricted to the husband's parents as the wife's parents are taken care of by her brothers. In most cases, male siblings take care of their ageing parents, and their better halves support such a noble cause.

A wife always respects her in-laws. Though many daily soaps exaggerate this relationship badly, in actuality, the mother-in-law and daughter-in-law are good friends. They share many more good moments than any other relationship in an Indian joint family. They share each other's work, help each other's necessities, and guide each other in different matters. Likewise, in my home, my wife has taught my mother how to handle a smart phone and social media accounts. My mother has taught her secret cooking styles. Not only my mother but also my father has learnt many technology-related things from my wife. They three are spending more time in home, sharing more ideas, experiences than me with my wife or my kid with his mother.

My wife is the caretaker of my parents, creator of my son, and supporter of my ideas. She has been shaping up my kid's future. She is the backbone of my family. Likewise, in any family, a wife plays the lead role in maintaining the family members' health and wealth. Their support system sticks the family members together, brings smile on everybody's face.

A good wife always forgives her husband when she's wrong.

-Milton Berle

Who, being loved, is poor?

- Oscar Wilde

**In a world full of temporary things,
you are a perpetual feeling.**

–Sanober Khan

She has been burying her emotions, sacrificing her ambitions to make you happy. Make your family happy.

All living objects have emotions. Emotion expresses the inner feelings. Emotion reflects on faces, activities, attitudes. Sharing self-emotion with the near and dear ones relaxes the mind, feel light-hearted. We share our emotions with friends, family members, relatives.

Different types of emotions are meant to be shared with different individuals, different close circles.

When we feel happy, we share our happiness with a larger group of people. When we are sad, we restrict our feelings to close ones. When we fail, we share our disheartened stories with our wives only. Because they can feel the hard work we put in, to succeed in that assignment. In a similar manner, they, too, are supposed to share their failure stories with us. But, unfortunately, a wife shares only good things with her husband. Bad experiences are generally absorbed by her. She finds it very difficult to express her emotions easily.

As a male individual, a husband enjoys his professional life with colleagues and his personal life with his wife and family members. But, an office-going wife is unable to enjoy her professional life with colleagues rather always thinks about her child, her husband, and her family members. Her mind roams around her child's school homework, husband's food likes, in-laws medicine reminders. A home maker is always busy in contributing her best towards family well-being.

We have seen Indian movies in which the mother used to keep the best food for her child, serve sufficient food to the family members, and, at last, consume the leftover portion. I have seen many times that my mother ate mine and my father's leftover food on a plate. That does not mean there was no food left or we were unable to provide for her. Rather, she didn't want to waste food. My wife has also been continuing the same practice.

A middle-class wife never throws half-used vegetable pieces rather keeps them in the refrigerator for next time use. She presses hard on the toothpaste tube so that the last drop of toothpaste can be used and not wasted. Similar in the case of toilet soaps, hair oil bottles, and body lotion containers. She stores the plastic food containers that are already used by restaurants to deliver food to our house. She stores each and everything where she feels that it has some future use.

A girl has some ambitions in her life. She wants to become like somebody, live like any of her ideal characters, and engage in any profession that will give her satisfaction. However, she fails to follow some of these desires due to marriage constraints. How big is the in-law's house, how much money does her husband earn, and how much support does she get from him. She can't fulfil all her dreams because she has to think about all her family members and give them enough time. She has to sacrifice her emotions many times to make her husband happy and make her family members happy.

Sacrifices are essential in a relationship because they show your partner that you care about them and their well-being. Relationships are a two-way street, and both partners must be willing to make sacrifices for each other. Sacrifices can come in many forms, such as giving up your time, compromising on decisions, or making financial sacrifices. Hence, only a wife shouldn’t bury her emotion. The husband also has to sacrifice his time, some of his personal preferences, to make his wife happy, make his family happy.

Making sacrifices is not easy at all. But it’s required for a happy and healthy relationship. When you make a sacrifice for your partner, it shows them that you are willing to put their needs before your own. This act of selflessness can strengthen the bond between you and your partner, leading to a more fulfilling relationship. Always remember, true love is selfless. It is prepared to sacrifice.

Many times, my wife says, "You never make time for me." It means, she wants to be heard, she wants to share her feelings, she wants to spend quality time with me. Likewise, we all men might have come across our wives' demand for not giving proper time to her. In such cases, what should we do?

The answer is simple. Take off from your office work and daily routines. Go for a vacation with her. If your kids are small, take them with you. If they have grown enough, leave them with your parents or in-laws. When you change the atmosphere and surroundings, wife's mind will recharge. It will strengthen the bond between you and her. She will feel how you care about her and how you have sacrificed your office routines and given time to her. Making sacrifices can lead to a more fulfilling relationship. When both husband and wife are willing to make sacrifices for each other, it creates a sense of balance and equality in the relationship. This can lead to a greater trust and intimacy between couples.

Many times, we use sacrifice as a synonym for compromise. In reality, both are not the same. Compromise is a situation where both partners give up something to reach a mutual agreement. However, sacrifices are more significant than compromises and often require one partner to make a bigger sacrifice than the other. In the Indian context, a wife always sacrifices in a broader way than any husband does in his whole lifetime. As a husband, we all should accept that, and respect their sacrifices, spend some quality time with them. If not every day, at least on weekends. Going to a movie with her, roaming in a park by holding her hand, and eating ice cream in a roadside stall can create magic in our association. It will recharge our relationship, make it smoother, heal the wife's heart, and make her feel better.

Of all the home remedies,
a good wife is best.

-Kin Hubbard

**Love looks not with the eyes,
but with the mind.**

- William Shakespeare

It has made me better loving you...
It has made me wiser, and easier,
and brighter.

- Henry James

She is your asset.
The moveable asset who does magic every day, uninterruptedly.

Everybody has some net worth. It's calculated by subtracting all liabilities from the total assets of an individual. Bankrupted people have a negative net worth. A worthy individual has a high net worth. Some get high-value assets by birth, some acquire them by work. Be it a salary earner, an entrepreneur, a politician, or a bureaucrat, everybody runs after money. All want to accumulate some wealth so that the next generation will enjoy it. In this wealth race, we, too, have been participating to secure our old age and our children's future.

Assets are categorised based on their nature - tangible assets, intangible assets, movable assets, immovable assets, current assets, non-current assets, quick assets, etc. In all these asset types, one thing is common: it has some book value. Some are keen on movable assets like a car or bike, some are doing charity to increase his or her goodwill. We Indians give more importance to fixed assets like land and buildings. Gen-Z believes in quick assets and enjoying their life instead of accumulating more than the required fixed assets.

A wife plays an important role in acquiring any type of asset in a husband's life. A wife always puts a break on expenditure, which is a good sign for any family. Because we male characters are very much interested in spending and give lesser importance to saving in general. We want to go to dine out every weekend with family members. Do parties with colleagues, replace old vehicles frequently, take a long vacation every year, etc. Meanwhile, our wives want to save money for our children's education, future uncertainties, and hospital emergencies. Even for their own purpose, women never spend freely, rather save for the future.

In our Indian culture, Goddess *Lakshmi* is being worshiped as lord of wealth. As per the *Hindu* calendar, everybody prays Goddess *Lakshmi* in different days, different functions. In Andhra Pradesh its *Varalakshmi Puja*, In Odisha its *Manabasa Gurubar*, In West Bengal its *Lokkhi Pujo*, In North India, its *Dhentaras*. Everybody prays God for good health and good wealth.

A dedicated wife always prays to God for her family's well-being and her child's future. She increases the value of any house by her behaviour in front of others. She maintains decorum in front of elders. She shows her dignity, which reflects the family's approach to the outer world. The child always learns from his or her mother, which in turn increases the value of any house. As a father, when I hear good things about my son's behaviour, I feel proud. I thank my wife for nurturing him nicely. Because of her meticulous involvement, my child's attitude and approach have become polite. His character is shaped thoroughly by my wife.

For me, my son is an asset. I have been sacrificing many small things for his big future dream which I see together, along with my wife. My wife has sacrificed her food, time, enjoyment for the career of our child. In compare with my dedication, her devotion and commitment is much more when it comes to our child's physical and mental growth.

All mothers' contribution towards their kids' growth and development are much more significant than those of any family member. A son likes his mother. A daughter likes her father. It's only a proverb. In actuality, both son and daughter like their mother. They are more acquainted with their mother than their father. The main reason behind this is time. Mother spends more time with them. From waking up in the morning to sleeping at night, a mother always prompts her children to follow the daily routine. She checks the school bag, helps with homework, and packs the tiffin box for her children. In parent-teacher meetings, the mother has a lot of questions to ask, and the father becomes a silent spectator because the mother follows the daily progress of the school syllabus thoroughly while the father is always busy with career opportunities.

A wife saves a lot of money for her husband. Many miscellaneous expenses are saved because of a wife's smart moves. She packs a tiffin career for her husband every working day, irons dresses of children, keeps an eye on unnecessary electricity consumption in the home, points out to the maid for better housekeeping, bargains with vegetable vendors and gets free coriander leaves. Her small contribution every day makes a big impact on her husband's pocket. She is the best money manager, who knows the perfect art of saving. She is a real asset who appreciates her value every day.

A middle class wife's make up budget is lesser than her child's tuition fees. She seldom goes to parlour. Her weekend outing may be fulfilled with a bunch of *panipuri* or an ice cream. She checks the price of a food item before ordering in any restaurant, carries baby water bottle to theatres for avoiding high charged packaged drinking water. She saves a lot for us.

In my opinion, a wife is worth deserving a gold jewellery every year based on the savings she makes and the sacrifices she makes during her whole lifetime. She never demands something for herself rather always refuses to accept any gifts and demotivates us while booking anything for her online. She really does magic for our financial strengths and should be respected for those same.

Love is not a feeling of happiness.
Love is a willingness to sacrifice.

- Michael Novak

No man succeeds without a good woman behind him. Wife or mother, if it is both, he is twice blessed indeed.

-Godfrey Winn

The greatest marriages are built on teamwork, mutual respect, a healthy dose of admiration, and a never-ending portion of love and grace.

– Fawn Weaver

She has sacrificed everything.
It's your turn to keep her wealthy,
both mentally and physically.

She gets married, accepts new family, becomes mother, sacrifices everything. She is the real example of the art of giving. For her dedication, contribution and hard work, it's the duty of any husband to keep his wife happy.

Happiness is of different types, namely - physical happiness, economic happiness, spiritual happiness, and emotional happiness. For different people, the priority of happiness differs, and the preference series changes. To feel happiness, a human being should follow various stages in his or her life. Those are motivation, energy, inspiration, planning, anticipation, satisfaction, pleasure, and gratitude. Change in the sequence of these steps can linger the happiness in anybody's life. The wife always follows these steps correctly to bring early happiness to all her family members' faces.

Now it's our turn to make our wives happy. As our relationship grows older, we become familiar with each other's habits, preferences, likes, dislikes easily and act accordingly. We should continue to support each other, respect each other's thought process for a healthier relationship. For keeping us mentally fit, we should take life easy, avoid the outsider's remark on our bond.

A husband and wife's attachment can't fade away easily. To avoid those external forces, we should train our minds positively. Any life has ups and downs. To enjoy each moment together, we should follow these six steps:

1. Managing Stress Levels.
2. Enjoying Each Other's Companionship
3. Boost Individual's Self Esteem
4. Follow A Healthy Lifestyle
5. Talk to Each Other
6. Be Resilience

Managing Stress Levels: The husband's overburdened office work and the wife's various household work often bring stress to the individual's mind. Once a person gets stressed, he or she explodes the individual's reaction. To manage those stress levels, it's better to leave the office atmosphere while at home. Avoid official phone calls after reaching home. Evening time is meant for family wellness. Share quality time with wife and children. Similar in the case of a working lady also. A homemaker is always ready to reduce her husband's stress because of her experience.

Enjoying Each Other's Companionship: Time heals. Spending quality time with each other reduces the sadness, brings smile on faces. Sitting beside your partner, watching a movie together, sharing your difficulties, reduces the stress level drastically and heals the heart promptly.

Boot Individual's Self-Esteem: Every person can do a miracle. An individual can go to an extreme level to make his or her life partner healthy, physically and mentally. The capability can be seen during hardship days. The dedication of a wife can be felt when her husband is in hospital. Similarly, when a wife falls sick, it's the duty of the husband to take leave from office work, switch off the mobile phone, bring her favourite food, and take care of the children. She should feel that you give her the utmost importance during her bad phases.

Follow a Healthy Lifestyle: Good food, good life. Bad habits suck life. An ideal wife always wants her husband to avoid outside food, smoking cigarettes, consuming alcohol and extramarital affairs. Our good habits save money, prolong our lifespan, and reflect goodness in our child's lifestyle. Due to work pressure or laziness, a wife sometimes forgets to take care of her health, not eat properly, and not sleep nicely. In such a situation, we should convince her and make her life easier.

Talk to Each Other: As we talk, we come to know each other better. Any relationship becomes stronger by sharing the words and verdicts between husband and wife. Holding her hand, waking in a park can evaporate the anger, heal the heart, and make the mind peaceful. Therefore, make it a habit to talk with your wife at least once during lunch break in your office and a few minutes after the children sleep at night. It will heal her mind and make her fit mentally.

Be Resilient: As a human being, she may react to silly things. It may be because of undue work pressure in the office or children's irritation at home. In such a situation, be resilient. Try to absorb her barking. It may last for a few minutes. Once she slows down, you try to explain. Better act as a mute spectator while she vomits out her anger. Once she feels relaxed, she will realise and praise your patience. This silence is the real support system for any healthy relationship.

Whoever is happy, makes others happy. A happy wife makes a happy home. A happy husband makes his wife happy. Happiness lies within our thought process, our own behaviours. We men should take an oath to make our wives happy. Celebrate wife's small achievements. Encourage her innovations. Discover her passions. Support her decisions. Then only a healthy relationship will be built. A strong connection will bloom between both. Our married life will become successful.

True love is selfless.
It is prepared to sacrifice.

- Sadhu Vaswani

The difference between an ordinary marriage and an extraordinary marriage is in giving just a little extra every day, as often as possible, for as long as we both shall live.

– Fawn Weaver

My wife is not just an option,
She is my priority.

-Padhi